School RULES!

WRITING

ideas, how-to's, and tips
to make you a whiz with words

by Emma MacLaren Henke
illustrated by Stacy Peterson

Published by American Girl Publishing

No part of this book may be used or reproduced
in any manner whatsoever without written permission except in the
case of brief quotations embodied in critical articles and reviews.

17 18 19 20 21 22 23 24 LEO 10 9 8 7 6 5 4 3 2 1

Editorial Development: Darcie Johnston
Art Direction & Design: Wendy Walsh
Production: Jeannette Bailey, Caryl Boyer, Virginia Gunderson, Cynthia Stiles
Illustrations: Stacy Peterson
Special thanks to Tanya Zempel, elementary education consultant

Library of Congress Cataloging-in-Publication Data

Names: Henke, Emma MacLaren, author. | Peterson, Stacy.
Title: School rules! Writing : ideas, how-to's, and tips to make you a whiz with words /
by Emma MacLaren Henke ; illustrated by Stacy Peterson.
Description: Middleton, WI : American Girl Publishing, [2017] |
Series: School rules! | Audience: 8+
Identifiers: LCCN 2016025283 (print) | LCCN 2016032717 (ebook) |
ISBN 9781683370000 (pbk.) | ISBN 9781683370031 (ebook) | ISBN 9781683370031 (epub)
Subjects: LCSH: Language arts (Secondary) | Language arts (Secondary)—Problems,
exercises, etc. | Language and languages—Study and teaching (Secondary)—
Problems, exercises, etc. | Second language acquisition. | BISAC: JUVENILE NONFICTION
/ Language Arts / General. | JUVENILE NONFICTION / Language Arts / Composition &
Creative Writing. | JUVENILE NONFICTION / School & Education.
Classification: LCC LB1631 .H36 2017 (print) | LCC LB1631 (ebook) | DDC 428.4071/2–dc23
LC record available at https://lccn.loc.gov/2016025283

Dear Reader,

Writing is one of your top tools for school. You put a lot of effort into your studies, and writing lets you show what you know. It lets you shine!

The advice and activities in this book will help you hone the writing skills you need for any kind of assignment, in any subject. You'll find tips on how to generate ideas and plan your writing as well as guidelines for stories, reports, essays, poems, and more. You may even get inspired to write on your own!

Writing is like a superpower. When you write, you can make anything happen. You can choose words and the ideas you're communicating with them. Your voice can be funny or passionate, angry or joyous. Your writing can teach, persuade, or inspire. Your words can change hearts and minds. Your words might even change the world.

The power is all yours.

your friends at American Girl

contents

GET READY TO WRITE

Perfect your process for a smooth start to any writing assignment.

WHERE DO IDEAS COME FROM?

What inspires you and sets your mind in motion?

WHEN YOU'RE WRITING A SHORT STORY?

a. thinking about the highlights of your favorite fantasy book series

b. remembering how you solved your last fight with your best friend

c. wondering what would happen if you could read people's minds

WHEN YOU'RE WRITING ABOUT CURRENT EVENTS?

a. talking about the news with your dad and mom

b. skimming the headlines on a news website

c. flipping through news magazines

WHEN YOU'RE WRITING A PERSONAL ESSAY ABOUT YOUR FAVORITE HOLIDAY MEMORY?

a. calling your grandma, who makes the world's best Thanksgiving dinner

b. browsing family photo albums

c. paging through your journal from the last year

when you're writing a book report?

a. listing books by authors you enjoy

b. wondering how a favorite character would solve your problems

c. asking your friends about the novels they love

when you're writing a history report about colonial america?

a. watching a documentary about colonial cooking

b. looking through your notes from history class

c. chatting with your mom about your family's trip to Colonial Williamsburg

when you're writing a haiku for your school literary magazine?

a. thinking about your favorite colors, sounds, and tastes

b. picking out details of an interesting photo or painting

c. listing words you love because of the way they sound

answers

As you might have guessed, they're all right answers! Your life, your experiences, and your thoughts are the best sources you have for writing ideas. School writing assignments usually give you a starting point, such as "Tell a story from your summer vacation" or "Write a poem about your favorite season." But most assignments leave plenty of room to imagine, research, and develop your own ideas.

LET IT POUR!

Brainstorm your way to a flood of ideas.

Suppose your teacher starts the school year by giving you this assignment:

School's out from June to September, but learning happens all year long! Write 3 to 5 paragraphs about something you learned over summer vacation.

Great! You went to summer camp, and you learned some new skills and made new friends. Plus, you spent a week with your grandpa, who taught you his favorite card games. You've got so many possibilities!

Brainstorming helps you choose a topic from all those possibilities and develop ideas for your writing projects. When you brainstorm, you scribble your thoughts quickly, without worrying about being neat or writing in complete sentences or wondering if they are *good* ideas. Just write down as many ideas as you can.

Check out the brainstorming techniques on the next few pages, and try one, two, or all three!

MIND MAP

Write your prompt, question, or topic at the center of a blank page and circle it. Then write any ideas inspired by the topic around it. Draw lines to connect the ideas to your topic—and to each other when they relate in some way.

Uncle Joey is a shark!

Pinochle

still need matches

Euchre

How to make Mom's famous Spongecake

Learned to make a campfire

Card tricks

During week with Grandpa

How to shuffle

What did I learn this summer?

Silly camp songs

Canoeing takes teamwork

Paddle to Eagle Island

Learned to canoe

At Summer Camp

J stroke C stroke

Don't stand up!

HIT LIST

Brainstorm ideas in the form of a list. Start by writing your topic at the top of the paper. Then divide the paper into three or four areas.

Next, start to brainstorm the main points or ideas you might want to explore, putting one idea at the top of each area you marked off. Leave plenty of room below each of those ideas to brainstorm and list your supporting points.

Learning to Canoe

MAIN IDEA 1: summer camp
- really wanted to go
- first time, needed tons of supplies
- didn't know girls in cabin

MAIN IDEA 2: canoe lessons
- embarrassed because everyone else knew what to do
- DON'T STAND UP!
- different strokes

MAIN IDEA 3: how I did it
- practice
- working with team
- Eagle Island!

PENCIL POINT

Boost your brainstorming by setting a timer for 5 or 10 minutes. Keep writing ideas until the timer beeps—without judging! Just write down anything that comes to mind as fast as you can. When you're done, look for the best ideas. There are some gold nuggets in there!

QUESTION YOURSELF

Take a look at your topic, and think about the basic questions you want to answer in your writing:

Who?

Why?

When?

Where?

What?

How?

Brainstorm answers (when you know them) and think of new questions, too.

Learning to Canoe

WHAT? learning to canoe

WHO? me, along with summer camp friends

WHERE? Camp Woodsy, on the lake

WHEN? this summer

WHY? wanted to try something new. Also, cabinmates all knew how and wanted me to canoe with them

HOW? lessons and practice

HOW did I FEEL?
-nervous at first, wanted to fit in
-embarrassed (fell out of canoe)
-proud to canoe to Eagle Island 🙂

TWO MORE QUESTIONS

Whichever brainstorm techniques you try, make sure to ask yourself two final questions:

1 What is the main idea I want to share?

2 What is my job or purpose for writing?

The first question is simple. It helps you choose the main idea you're going to write about before you actually start writing.

WHAT IS THE MAIN IDEA I WANT TO SHARE?
I want to tell the story of how I learned to canoe.

The second question is a bit trickier. The purpose of your writing is the job you want it to do. It's the *why*.

Writing can do lots of jobs, but three of the most important are to . . .

Persuade, Inform, and Entertain. Think PIE. Mmmm...

Good Writing

MAIN IDEA

PURPOSE

A "piece" of writing (think PIE!) can do any or all of these jobs. For instance, a newspaper article about the weather informs. A story about a magical princess who uses her powers for good might entertain and persuade. A book review informs and persuades. Think about your purpose before you begin writing.

WHAT IS MY PURPOSE FOR WRITING?
I want to show how I learned to canoe.
(I want to INFORM.)

I think how I learned to canoe makes a good story.
(I want to ENTERTAIN.)

As you move forward, keep your main idea and purpose in mind to keep your writing on the right track!

order, order
Use outlines to organize your ideas.

Making an **outline** helps you put your ideas in order before you start writing. Think of it as a map showing how you'll connect your brainstorm ideas, moving from the beginning of your piece to the end. When you start writing, the outline will keep you from getting stuck and wondering what should come next.

Here's how:

 Look at your brainstorm notes and decide which order to put your main ideas in—from first to last, from beginning to middle to end.

 Write each main idea in order and number it, leaving lots of space between the main ideas. Use just enough words to understand each idea. You don't need to write in neat, complete sentences!

 Under each numbered main idea, add points that support it, in the order that makes the most sense. Put a letter in front of each. If any of *those* points have supporting points, write them under their lettered point.

How I Learned to Canoe

1. new at summer camp

    a. my first time there, but others had been before

    b. made friends in my cabin

    c. my friends wanted to canoe, but I'd never done it

2. canoe lessons

    a. learned different strokes

    b. most important rule: don't stand up

    c. but I did stand, and I fell!

        —sooo embarrassed

        —determined to learn

3. canoe success!!!

    a. kept practicing every day

    b. last day, canoe trip to Eagle Island
       with friends

        —super fun!

        —proud of myself :)

PENCIL POINT

All writing tells a story. Outlining helps you figure out the story you're going to tell. You think about which ideas are more important than others, and you choose which ones come first, second, and third, all the way to the end. Remember those two big questions? *What is the main idea I want my writing to share?* and *What's my purpose for writing, the job I want my writing to do?* Outlining helps you answer them. It also helps you feel ready and maybe even excited to tell your story. Let the writing begin!

17

CRAFT YOUR DRAFT

Put pen to paper
or fingers to keyboard
and let the words flow!

WHERE can you write RIGHT?

Find your best setting for getting down to work.

1

You keep your desk at home . . .

full of photos, knickknacks, and desk toys you can fidget with.

completely clutter free. When you sit down to work, you set out the exact materials you'll need.

in front of your bedroom window. You love to look at the beautiful trees, birds, and sunsets.

2

You'd do your best on a test . . .

at a private study table in the silence of the school library.

surrounded by your class-mates, whom you could see working hard.

if you knew you could ask questions and get up to stretch for a break.

PENCIL POINT

Writing takes inspiration and concentration. Find a spot that has the right mix for you!

3

When you have an online homework assignment, you're likely to . . .

keep your e-mail open so you can get help from friends as you work.

be distracted clicking on the hilarious kitten videos your sister told you about.

visit only your class website and the pages you use to find the information you need.

When you study, you listen to . . .

your favorite music in the background. The beat keeps your mind moving and makes study time speed by.

the sounds of your home, such as your brother chatting on the phone while your dad cooks dinner in the kitchen. You take mini-breaks to listen in or taste dad's progress.

nothing! You like a quiet space.

Your class is reading a novel, you're behind, and you've got to finish by tomorrow! You'd settle down to read . . .

wherever you are. But you'd ask people to make sure you keep turning those pages.

in that comfy beanbag chair in your attic. No one will bother you up there!

at your kitchen table. Your mom will keep you on track, and you can stop for a snack anytime you like.

Answers

Did you pick mostly **purple** answers? You may write best in a space away from distractions, such as your room or a quiet spot at the library. You need to find focus in order to work. If you have a hard time concentrating around noise, try wearing earplugs or noise-canceling headphones.

Did you choose **red** the most? You look for motivation in what-ever is around you. You could be comfortable any place you find inspiring. Maybe you'd like a group setting, such as a writing center or study hall. Try creating playlists of motivating music for the times you need to work on your own.

Did you go for **green?** You prefer a writing space that lets you take time-outs when you need them. Whether you're working at home or away, plan breaks into your work time. But be careful not to let the breaks take over!

21

scribe supplies

Stock your desk with these top tools for writing.

pens
Use colors to inspire yourself!

pencils

dictionary
Not sure you're using a word correctly or spelling it right? Look it up!

Standard Dictionary

computer
Use it for both writing and research.

style manual
You'll need a guide to great grammar and fabulous formatting.

Pocket Style Manual NEW

Sarah Murphy
English

Once upon a time there was a....

paper

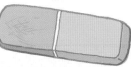

library card
Writers read!
Writers do research!

erasers
Use an engineer's or artist's eraser to keep your work neat.

sticky notes
Make notes in books or on your own work with these removable wonders.

thesaurus
Add variety to your writing with fresh words and phrases.

highlighters
Highlight important passages on printouts or photocopies. When you're reviewing your own words, highlight passages you love—or passages you'd love to change.

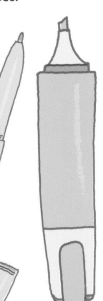

notebooks
Use full-size notebooks for projects or journal writing. Carry a small notebook with you to write your thoughts when inspiration strikes.

keystroke or pen stroke?

What's the best way for *you* to start writing?

Your teacher may ask for a "handwritten" or "typed" paper in the assignment directions. Until you create the final version, though, what you use to write your words is completely up to you. Pen or keyboard—which helps your words flow? Consider the pluses and the minuses of high-tech versus hands-on writing.

PROS / CONS

Pen and Paper

Pros:

You can take a notebook anywhere you go!

It's satisfying to hold your writing in your hands.

You'll never run out of battery power.

You don't have to share a notebook with someone else who might need to use it.

Cons:

Fixing mistakes, revising sentences, and rearranging your thoughts take more time and effort.

You have to recopy and rewrite your words for each new draft.

If your writing gets lost or destroyed, you don't have a backup.

Computer

Pros:

Typing can be faster than writing by hand.

It's easy to move, copy, cut, and paste your words in a computer document.

It's easy to back up your work so that you never lose a word.

Spell-check!

Cons:

Computers are expensive. You probably have to share a computer at home or school, and your time on it may be limited.

Computers connect you to a world of distractions, such as games and online videos.

Your computer might not be located in your favorite study spot.

write now!

These dos and don'ts will help you start your draft,
even when you feel stuck.

DO brainstorm and outline before you start writing your draft. When you work from an outline, you won't waste time wondering what you're going to write next.

DO keep the assignment sheet with all the instructions and requirements close by. Also, remember those important questions: *What is the main idea I want my writing to share? What job do I want my writing to do?* Use the assignment and questions to guide your writing and help you focus.

DON'T feel like you have to write the entire draft all at once. Give yourself time to write—and time *not* to write. If you set aside your writing for a day, you might discover that your words are better than you remembered!

DO try free writing. If you feel like you can't come up with the right words, write whatever comes to mind on your topic for 5 or 10 minutes. It doesn't matter what words you choose or whether you want to keep your ideas. Just move your pencil across the paper until time's up.

DON'T sit there staring at a blank screen or page for more than a few minutes. Try free writing or a new brainstorming technique. Reread your assignment, searching for clues to focus your writing. Take a jumping-jacks break!

DON'T get mad at yourself if you get stuck. *You can do it!* Writing isn't a special gift. It's a skill that just takes planning, practice, and persistence—three things that everyone can do.

FEELING BLOCKED?

Try these timely tactics to get your pencil moving.

✳ **Check in with a friend.** Set up a time to review each other's assignments well before the due date.

✳ **Reward yourself.** Build small breaks and treats into your writing time. Finish a page? Get a glass of water, stretch, or play with your pet. Write for an hour? Take a quick cocoa break. Choose rewards that work for *you*.

✳ **Talk out loud** and record your writing if you're tired of typing or writing by hand. Most smartphones, tablets, and computers can record what you say.

✳ **Set a timer** for 15 or 20 minutes, and keep writing until you hear the beep. Don't stop to get a snack or chat with your sister. Just write. Do this in manageable chunks until you're finished.

✳ **Set small writing goals** before you begin. Decide you're going to write a certain number of words, paragraphs, or pages, and don't stop until you've done it. You'll feel great when you reach your goal!

Practice Makes
. . . a Habit

The more you write, the better you write and the easier writing becomes. Here's how to make writing a habit.

Keep a journal. Every day write a bit about something that happens to you or something you notice. Write about your impressions. Write about feeling excited or uncomfortable. Write about disappointments and delights. Write about feeling bored. Just write a little bit at a time, as often as you can.

Take note of your ideas. Inspiration can strike anytime, anywhere. Carry a small notebook with you to capture your best ideas as soon as they come to mind.

Make lists. List your favorite words and expressions. List situations that make you nervous. List funny things your friends have told you. List your hopes and dreams. You can list whatever you like! Later, use your lists to inspire new writing projects.

Listen. Pay attention to conversations among your friends and family. Set aside time to go places where you're sure to overhear people talking, such as the bookstore, a park or playground after school, or the bleachers before your team's game. Write notes about what you hear. Use real-life conversations to inspire your fiction stories and to add new perspectives to your essays and reports.

Ask questions and answer them. When you're wondering about something, write down your question. Then search for an answer. Or make up your own answer! Curiosity sparks writing.

DON'T BE A COPYCAT

Credit your sources, and put ideas in your own words.

Copying the writing or ideas of others and presenting them as your own is called **plagiarism.** You know that plagiarism is wrong, but when you're researching a project, it can be confusing to figure out exactly what counts as copying.

Some cases of plagiarism are clear-cut:
• Copying wording from a book or magazine and presenting it as your own.
• Cutting and pasting passages from websites into your report.
• Using a quote from an expert without giving that person credit.

Other times, it's harder to tell. When in doubt, here's what to do:
• When you use ideas that are not your own, give **credit** to your source.
• When you're writing facts and findings about a topic, **paraphrase** the information—which means put it into your own words.

HOW TO STEER CLEAR

Make a list. When you're reading books, websites, articles, and other materials for a writing project, keep a list of your sources.

Practice paraphrasing. Read your source material. Then set it aside while you make notes about the main ideas from the source, using your own words.

Mark quotes. When you copy information from a source into your research notes, put quotation marks around the information and write "QUOTE" next to it.

Trust your gut. Plagiarism is about right and wrong. Do what you know is right—or ask a teacher. If you make a mistake or forget to credit a source, fix it and learn from it.

EXTRA CREDIT

Do you know when credit is due?

You're researching your report on canoeing, and you find a helpful website called *CanYouCanoe.com*. Read this passage from the site and the three statements that follow, and then decide whether each statement is **copy smart** or **copycat**.

http://www.canyoucanoe.com/you-too

YOU TOO CAN CANOE!

Humans have been paddling canoes for thousands of years. You can do it, too!

If you want to learn, take lessons from a canoe teacher. Better yet, ask an experienced paddler friend to join you in the boat and show you the strokes.

What's the first rule of canoeing for beginners? Don't stand up! That's a sure way to tip the boat over and fall in the water.

Next you need to know that the paddler sitting in the stern—or rear of the boat—steers the canoe and helps power it forward. The paddler in the bow—or front of the boat—mainly helps to move the boat forward.

1. According to CanYouCanoe.com, canoes have been around since long before European settlers came to America.

2. If you want to learn how to canoe, take lessons. Or, it's even better to ask an experienced paddler to show you the strokes.

3. Which paddler has the power when there are two in a canoe? "The paddler sitting in the stern—or rear of the boat—steers the canoe," says CanYouCanoe.com.

ANSWERS

1. **Copy Smart.** This sentence gives credit to the source for the information that canoes have been around a long time but states the idea in a new way.

2. **Copycat.** This sentence uses the same words as the original passage without giving credit.

3. **Copy Smart.** These sentences quote and credit the passage correctly.

SAY IT WITH STYLE

How you say it is as important
as *what* you say.

vIBranT voice

The voice of your writing shows how you feel about your topic—and about your audience.

Would you explain your science project with the same feelings you would use to describe your best friend? Probably not. Would you talk to your school principal the same way you talk to your little brother? No way! **Voice** is the writing tool you use to show that difference in both feeling and formality.

When you think about what voice to give a piece of writing, ask yourself:

What job does my writing need to do?

Who am I writing for?

Some tasks call for writing that's casual and might even feel like a conversation. For example, what voice would you use in a note to your BFF thanking her for helping you study?

<messages>

Hey Melanie!

Thanks for helping me practice for the spelling bee.
The buzz is you're the best friend ever!

See ya soon,
Aziza

Other writing jobs require a more formal voice. For instance, think about a thank-you letter you might write to your doctor after you spent the day shadowing her to learn about her job:

Dear Dr. Craig,

Thank you so much for giving me the chance to spend the day at your office. Watching you taught me a lot about what it takes to be a pediatrician.

Keep in mind your **audience**—the people you're "talking to" in your writing—to help you decide what kind of voice to use. If you want to experiment with voice, try changing the **perspective.** That is, change the person who's telling the story.

Imagine how different a story about your school might sound if it were written from your perspective, or from your teacher's perspective, or from the perspective of a new student. Changing perspective can help you find the specific voice you need for fiction, a report, a poem, or any other kind of writing.

Changing perspective also gives you freedom with words. A villain or a queen might say things that *you* would never dare to!

PENCIL IN PERSONALITY

Decide the right voice for the job.

The writing jobs in each pair below might seem similar. If you look more closely, though, you can see that they need different voices. What kind of words would you use for each job? Would they be formal or informal? Funny or serious? Joyful or reflective? Calm or passionate? Full of feeling or just the facts?

Write a letter to your grandma.

Write a letter to the President.

Write a poem about Halloween fun.

Write a poem about how Halloween reminds you of your big sister, who's away at college.

Write a report on how your favorite candy bar is made.

Write a report on how a vaccine is made.

Write an essay arguing for a later bedtime.

Write an essay arguing for a lower voting age.

Write a book report about a funny graphic novel.

Write a book report about a biography of Harriet Tubman.

write a road map

Give clear directions to help readers
follow your writing from beginning to end.

IN THE BEGINNING

A great beginning captures your reader's attention.
Use a **hook** to draw in your audience and make them
eager to read all the way through. Try starting with . . .

a question: Get your reader wondering about your topic from the very first sentence.

> How long have humans kept cats as pets? A few hundred years? A thousand years? Some scientists say . . .

a cool fact: A unique tidbit of information engages your reader's mind.

> Some scientists believe people have kept cats as pets for as long as 12,000 years!

a quote: Let an expert or well-known person make your point right away.

> Mark Twain once said, "If man could be crossed with a cat, it would improve man but it would deteriorate the cat."

a joke or clever idea: If you make your reader smile, she'll feel good about your piece and stick with it.

> Why do cats make terrible storytellers? They have only one tail! So let me tell you all about them instead.

dialogue: In fiction, starting with a conversation drops readers immediately into the action.

> "Oh Nosey," sighed Ella, "you are the cleverest cat. If only you could talk and I could know what you're thinking!"
> "All you ever had to do was ask," Nosey purred in reply.

a statement of belief: Let your reader know how you feel about your subject right away so that she'll want to discover your reasoning.

> No doubt about it, cats make the best pets.

FOLLOW ME!

Words and phrases called **transitions** lead your reader from one part of the text to the next. Use transitions to signal . . .

the order of your ideas:
to begin, first, to start, next, afterward

changes in time:
after, next, as soon as, when, then, immediately, following that

difference in ideas:
in contrast, on the other hand, however, otherwise, although, nevertheless, but

location:
across, among, above, beyond, by, throughout

comparison:
in the same way, likewise, similarly, just like, as with

additional supporting information:
for instance, for example, also, in addition

PENCIL POINT

Strong beginnings, transitions, and endings strengthen the flow of storytelling in any kind of writing. If you tell a good story—even in a book report or poem or essay—your reader will stick with you.

emphasis:
for this reason, to repeat, importantly, again

conclusion or summary:
in conclusion, to sum up, as a result, in short

IN THE END

A strong conclusion sums up the points you made, lets readers form an opinion about your ideas, and answers any questions that you raised. Your ending should feel like an ending!

For reports and essays, write endings that . . .

restate your main idea—that is, say what you said in your introduction:
Cats make the best pets for many reasons.

remind readers of your evidence or supporting points:
Cats are friendly, they're happy living inside, and spending time with them can make you feel calm and happy.

answer questions you have asked or prompted the reader to ask:
If you're wondering whether a cat is the right pet for you, spend some time visiting cats at your local animal shelter. You might find a purr-fect friend.

For fiction or personal narrative, write endings that . . .

resolve the problems or conflicts in your story:
Finally, Ella and Nosey were safe, back at home, and curled together on their favorite chair.

leave readers with the feeling that your story is complete, even if all questions aren't answered and all problems aren't solved:
Ella knew Nosey would be her best friend forever, even if she didn't know how that cat learned to talk.

In any ending, it helps to remind your reader where you started. Think of it this way: If your writing is a circle, the ending closes the circle. If you started with a question, end with a well-supported answer. If you started with a character's experience, let her reflect on her experience. Circling back to the place you began can give your reader a feeling of satisfaction or completion.

WEIGH YOUR WORDS

Writing is a balancing act between words that are interesting and words that are clear.

SPICY SYNONYMS

When you're trying to find just the right word, turn to a **thesaurus.** Thesaurus words can spice up your writing and keep you from repeating yourself.

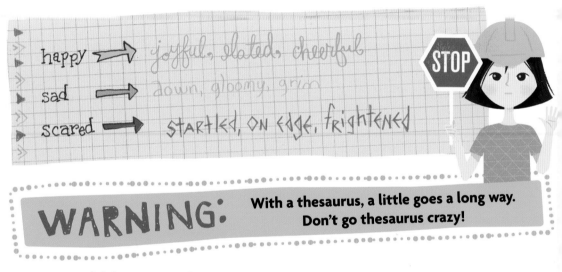

happy ➡ joyful, elated, cheerful
sad ➡ down, gloomy, grim
scared ➡ startled, on edge, frightened

WARNING: With a thesaurus, a little goes a long way. Don't go thesaurus crazy!

Adolescent pupils excel in their academic pursuits when the commencement of their daily erudition is postponed.

That's a pretty awful sentence, right? This one communicates the same idea:

Middle school students learn better when their school day starts later.

When you use a thesaurus, make sure you understand the full meaning of the words you choose. Don't be fooled by big, fancy-sounding words. They don't make writing sound any smarter!

TOO TIRED

Want to perk up your prose?
Try to find alternatives to these overused words.

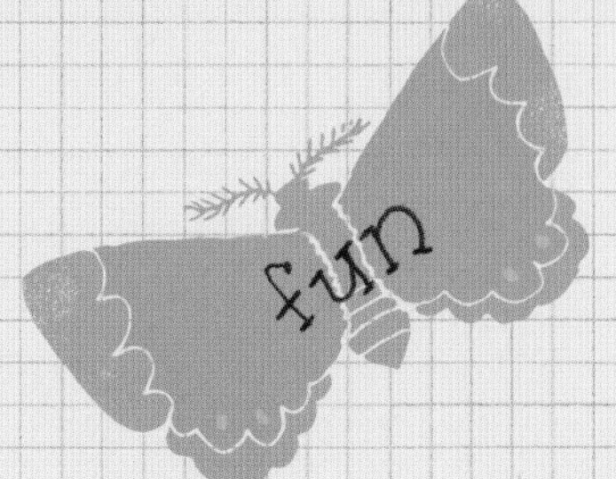

fun

very

things

went

good

interesting

cool

get

bad

great

really

a lot

stuff

pretty

cute

nice

Reserve standbys like these for times when
you actually *want* to be vague.

VIVID Verbs

Verbs show what's happening!
They're the engines that power your writing.
Try not to rely on *is*, *was*, and other forms of the verb *to be*. Instead, choose
verbs like these that give your writing power and emotion.

Amuse

Badger

Cajole

Dodge

Energize

Flush

Gush

Hush

Ignite

Jostle

Kindle

Loathe

Mystify

Neglect

Obscure

Ponder

Quip

Relish

Spy

Taunt

Upend

Verify

Wheeze

X-ray

Yearn

Zip

Come up with your own list of verbs with verve. Use the alphabet as inspiration,
or list verbs by category. Brainstorm verbs that show excitement, happiness,
distress, suspense—whatever you like!

Metaphor Magic

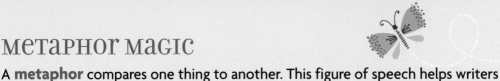

A **metaphor** compares one thing to another. This figure of speech helps writers describe someone or something in more interesting ways than by just using adjectives. Metaphors help readers imagine and feel what writers are telling them.

Instead of . . .

> Her feet felt tired and heavy after the walk-a-thon for the animal shelter.

a metaphor lets you say . . .

> Her feet were heavy bricks after the walk-a-thon for the animal shelter.

Instead of . . .

> When she thought about the recital, Lucy felt nervous, excited, petrified, confident, and sick all at the same time.

a metaphor lets you say . . .

> Riding the roller coaster of her feelings about the recital made Lucy feel sick to her stomach.

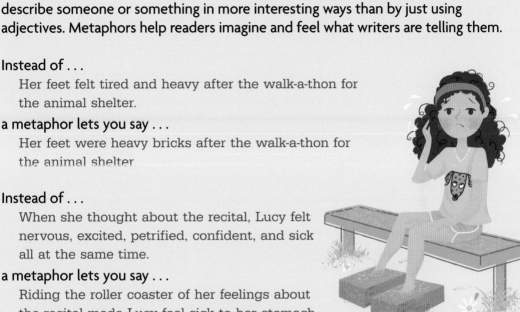

SPIFF IT UP

Metaphors aren't just for creative writing like fiction and poetry. They can add sparkle to any assignment or style of writing. Try adding a few to your next essay, report, or letter.

A **simile** is a certain kind of metaphor that compares two different things using the word *like* or *as*.

> After Claire made the winning basket, her face beamed as brightly as the sun.

> Corinne guarded her last piece of chocolate like precious gold.

POINTED PARAGRAPHS AND SENTENCE STYLE

Build strong paragraphs and sentences to give your ideas a solid foundation.

The purpose of a paragraph is to communicate a single idea. Whether you're writing fiction, an essay, or a report, each paragraph should contain one main point and the information that supports or relates to that point.

Sometimes beginning writers stuff too many thoughts into one paragraph. When in doubt, "unpack" your paragraphs. Think of it as breaking your writing down into smaller packages.

PENCIL POINT

Always indent when you begin a new paragraph in your writing.

Indent again when you begin the next paragraph, just like this.

Then don't forget to indent every new paragraph that you start—every time!

Sentences are the building blocks of paragraphs. Just like using a variety of words makes your writing more interesting, varying the way you put sentences together also helps readers want to keep reading.

Some sentences are short and straight to the point:

> We ate dinner.
>
> The dog ran down the street.
>
> Robins migrate with the seasons.

Some sentences combine more than one action or idea:

> We ate dinner and then watched a movie.
>
> The dog ran down the street, and then it stopped to sniff a flower at the bottom of the big oak tree.
>
> Robins fly south in the fall but return north again when spring arrives.

Paragraphs have a pleasing rhythm when they have both kinds of sentences instead of just one kind.

Take a look at these two paragraphs. Which one do you prefer?

> We hiked. We were hungry. We ate dinner. We watched a movie. It was funny. We were tired. We went to bed early.
>
> We felt hungry after our hike, so we ate dinner right away. Then we relaxed by watching a movie. It was really funny! We were tired, though, and went to bed early.

These short paragraphs tell the same basic information. But the first paragraph feels like a grocery list, while the second one feels like a . . .

STORY

creative and personal writing

Get inspired for
fiction, poetry, memoirs,
and more.

strong words

What are your writing strengths? Take this quick quiz to find out.

Your teacher assigns a current events report. You'd probably . . .

write about how a story from the news impacts you and your family.

visit the library to learn more about a headline that catches your eye.

scan the opinion pages in the newspaper or on news websites for inspiration.

focus your attention on a news piece that tells a fascinating story about a community hero.

When you're playing truth or dare, you like to . . .

choose "truth," but then make up a fib about yourself to see if you can fool your friends.

choose "dare." You can always argue your way out of it if the dare is too terrifying for your taste.

decide between "truth" and "dare" based on who's asking the question. If you think about what the person might ask before you choose, you're usually safe.

choose "truth." You love to tell stories about yourself, even the embarrassing ones.

You'd find it easiest to write about . . .

your favorite memory.

your favorite novel.

your favorite good cause.

your favorite animal.

Group project! You'd be an in-demand partner for a project in which you . . .

interview oldest family members and write about the experience.

report on the history of your city.

write and perform a skit.

persuade your peers to change your class rules.

You're most likely to watch a show about . . .

how the brain processes information.

zombies attacking the planet!

real people working hard to change their community for the better.

kids taking over their school.

Did you choose **blue** the most? You're probably comfortable with personal writing and not afraid to open up about yourself. Besides, what do you know more about than *you*? You like projects such as memoirs, poetry, and personal essays that let you express your feelings.

Did you select mostly **red?** You love stories—your own and everyone else's. Whether or not your writing is inspired by reality, you probably feel comfortable writing fiction. When you're making it up, the words just flow.

Did you go with **green?** You like subjects you can research and the challenge of putting your own spin on information. You probably feel most comfortable writing reports and informational essays.

Did you pick mostly orange? You like to voice your opinion and persuade. You shine with essays, reviews, and even advertisements. You love using words to convince others to see things your way.

Whatever answers you chose, you can use your strength in any kind of writing, whether your purpose is to persuade, to inform, to entertain, or to do all three. Start from your comfort zone, and grow as a writer in all areas!

MOUNTAIN CLIMBING

Take your readers for a climb!

Problems, or **conflicts,** are at the heart of fiction writing. They drive the action of a story, because they lay out what characters must do or try to do. Also, readers want to find out how the characters solve their problems.

When you're planning a story, come up with interesting conflicts to captivate your readers. Then use a "story mountain" technique to outline the plot from beginning to end.

Beginning

Introduce your main problem. What does your character want? What's standing in her way or holding her back? How will she prepare for the "climb"? If you're writing about a character your age, your main conflict could involve . . .

- fitting in at school.
- making the grade
  (or the team, or the cast, etc.).
- handling a big change.

Middle

Your character should face obstacles and other problems as you write your way up the mountain. Consider this: A mountain is not like a staircase—you don't climb straight up, never veering from the path. Your character may get sidetracked while she's trying to resolve her main conflict. Think of smaller problems as twists and turns in the path. These problems might be . . .

- a bad grade.
- a recipe that goes wrong.
- a fight with a friend.

Climax

You've made it to the peak! The **climax** is the point in the story when your character has to overcome or deal with the big conflict you set up at the beginning. This is usually the most exciting or tense part! Now your character might . . .

- face that scary tryout or test.
- finally get her moment in the spotlight.
- work through a crisis with the person who caused the conflict.

End

The problem is solved. Your character either gets what she hoped for or doesn't—or maybe she gets something even better. Or, she could get what she wants, only to discover she doesn't want it after all. Whatever happens, your character has changed or learned something as a result of the problem and its resolution. What she learns is your story's lesson, or **theme.** Your character might discover that . . .

- she had the smarts, talent, or confidence to make the grade (or the team or the cast) all along.
- true friendships are valuable.
- people's differences are what make them interesting and wonderful.

WHAT YOU SAY IS WHAT YOU GET

Spotlight conversation for powerful storytelling.

Use dialogue to **reveal your characters.** What's better than describing Cara with the words "nervous" and "superstitious"? Let her show it with her *own* words:

Ta-Da!

"I just have a feeling I'm going to blow it," Cara worried as she picked at her cuticle.

"My horoscope said, 'Beware! You may soon find yourself on the brink of disaster.'"

"You know those are baloney, right?" Mom replied.

"Yeah, I guess. But I still feel terrified to step on that stage."

Use dialogue to **advance the action** of your story. When you let the characters tell what's happening around them and behind the scenes, you draw interest to important information:

"I can't believe it!" gushed Cara. "I got the part!"

"I knew you could do it," confided her mom. "Now you've got to figure out how to memorize all those lines."

Use dialogue to **add conflict** or create tension. Writing dialogue to show how your characters interact when they face problems adds excitement and makes the characters feel alive:

"Break a leg. Literally," hissed Selena.

"Wait, what?" replied Cara to her understudy.

"Good luck, I mean."

"Sure you do," mumbled Cara. "That's just what I need," she thought.

FLOWING Format

These dialogue conventions will help your readers know who's saying what.

❝❝ Use quotation marks to set off words that are spoken.

❝❝ For words that characters think but don't say out loud, use either quotation marks or *italics*.

❝❝ Make a new, indented paragraph for each new speaker. Even if a character says only one word, that one word gets its own paragraph.

PENCIL POINT

Read your dialogue out loud. Does it sound authentic? Does it sound like real speech your characters would say? If the answer is no, rewrite it.

Say What?

When you write dialogue, try out these alternatives to the word *said*.

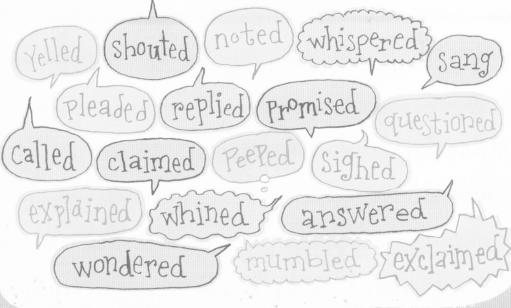

Yelled · Shouted · noted · whispered · sang · pleaded · replied · promised · questioned · Called · claimed · Peeped · sighed · explained · whined · answered · wondered · mumbled · exclaimed

FILL THE PAGE

Stuck for a story starter? Ponder these prompts.

Take a look at your favorite family photo. Come up with a not-quite-true story about what's going on in the picture.

Imagine you find a four-leaf clover that brings good luck.

Imagine your teacher leads a double life—math maven by day, spy by night!

What would happen if you suddenly discovered that you could no longer keep a secret?

Imagine your bus takes a detour and you never arrive at school.

What if your big sister became a famous pop star?

What happens when, returning from a family trip, the plane leaves without you but your family is onboard?

What if your bike was stolen?

What if you could read your mother's mind, but no one believed in your special ability?

Imagine your best friend starts wearing hats all the time. She won't take them off, ever! Why not?

Think of the last time you felt frustrated or defeated. What happened? Rewrite the situation so you come out on top.

What if you got locked in your school overnight?

Imagine you win a pony in a contest.

What if your family and friends forgot your birthday?

PLAYFUL POETRY

Poetry frees you to have fun with your words.

Poetry can rhyme
(but it doesn't have to):

Dribble fast, bounce it low.
Steal the ball. Quick! Let it go!
Shooting hoops on the court,
Wish I was tall, but I am short.

Poetry lets you experiment with the
sounds of language:

Slippery slope sliding down down down,
Hands high, waving skyward,
Moving faster till my feet fly out—
And stop me!

When you repeat words or emphasize
certain words, syllables, or sounds,
poetry has rhythm:

Miss Mary Mack, Mack, Mack,
All dressed in black, black, black,
With silver buttons, buttons, buttons,
All down her back, back, back.

Poems are the perfect place to practice using vivid verbs, clever metaphors, and other **well-chosen words:**

Detective on the playground,
Looking out for clues.
Hide-and-seek compels me—
The game I hate to lose!

alliteration is when words begin with the same sound:

jump jiving
sifting sand

assonance is when words have the same vowel sound:

fast laughter
even field

consonance is when words have the same consonant sound:

quick kicking
whisper spreading

57

pen your own poems

Not sure where to start? Try these familiar forms to make your poetry flow.

In an **acrostic** poem, the first letter of each line spells a name or word:

Relax, it's time to run!

Everyone!

Come along!

Each kid playing, having fun,

Side by

Side.

Try a **haiku**, a Japanese form of short poetry. The first line has five syllables, the next line has seven, and the last line has five. Haiku create a vivid sensory image with just a few words:

I swing high until
My toes touch the shining sun,
Then I fall away.

Write poems using **quatrains.** These are four-line **stanzas,** or sections, with rhyming words at the ends of the lines. Different styles of quatrains have different rhyme patterns.

The first two and second two lines might rhyme:

> We play four square every day.
> Bouncing, slapping balls in play.
> We smile, we laugh, we even shout—
> But one missed hit and you'll be out!

Or every other line might rhyme:

> Flying kites behind the school,
> Colors soaring through the sky.
> Wind gusts blowing strong and cool
> Speed the shapes and make them fly.

Come up with quatrains in whatever rhyme pattern suits you. If you're having trouble making rhymes, try choosing a different pattern.

Still stuck? Think of your favorite poem or poet. Try writing an extra verse to a song you love. Imitate or change a familiar poem to practice your poetry skills.

PENCIL POINT

Just like all writing, poetry has a job to do. It can tell a story. It can express emotions. It can describe an experience of the senses. Knowing which job (or jobs) you want your poem to do will help the words flow.

PICTURE THIS

Use your own poetic language to write about these images.

PENCIL POINT

Try to use the vivid language of poetry in everything you write. Delicious turns of phrase add flavor to stories, essays, reports, and letters, too!

WRITING ABOUT YOURSELF

Share your own stories.

Have you ever heard this piece of writing advice: "Write what you know"? What do you know more about than yourself? A **memoir** is a piece of writing you create to tell a story from your own life. In a **personal essay,** you share your feelings about a topic or situation based on your own experiences.

One reason teachers assign personal writing is to help you practice storytelling. You can learn that successful stories have conflict and resolution by writing about your own problems or challenges and how you overcame them.

Personal writing is also a great way to practice description. The characters and setting come from your memory, not your imagination. That means the details are real and in your mind, waiting for you to write them down.

My Life

LOOKING BACK

To prepare for your next personal writing assignment, use these prompts to uncover your life stories:

- Tell about a time you were really, really surprised.

- Tell about a big disappointment.

- Describe your happiest moment from today. Describe the happiest moment from the last year. Describe the happiest day of your life.

- Tell about a time you felt scared.

- What makes you laugh? What makes you cry? Why?

- Who is your favorite person? What makes this person so special to you?

- Tell about a time you made a difficult decision.

- Tell about a time you were brave.

- Explain how you are different now from the way you were one year ago.

- Compare a time you failed and a time you succeeded. What did you learn about yourself from each situation?

PENCIL POINT

What's one quick way to uncover stories about problems and solutions from your own life? Ask yourself, *What did I learn, and how did I learn it?* The question has a built-in conflict, or struggle. You begin with a problem: You don't know something you want to know. The story of how you learn is the solution to that problem.

HEEELP!
I HATE WRITING
ABOUT MYSELF!

Some stories are private! How would you feel if your teacher read your diary? What if she read it out loud to the entire class?!

Worries like these can make you freeze up when it's time to write about yourself. But it might help you relax if you can remember that personal writing helps you practice storytelling and description, and that's why your teacher has given you the assignment. Your teacher would not want you to share something you're not comfortable with.

Try these tactics to make personal writing feel a little *less* personal:

Talk to your teacher.

Can I talk to you about our assignment? I have a story to write, but it's private. I just want to make sure we won't be sharing this assignment in class or editing each other's work.

Write about your successes and happy times. Think of stories that you're proud to share.

Talk about your talents and skills. How did you learn to play the cello or win that karate tournament? You'll have a problem and a solution without delving into the details of your family or private life.

Write about your observations instead of private stories. Rather than sharing the embarrassing details of the time the teacher read a note you passed in class, write your opinions about passing notes in class. Instead of talking about your beloved pet that passed away, write about why pets are so important to you.

persuasive writing

Follow this formula for words that pop with the power of persuasion.

When you write a persuasive essay, letter, or speech, you're trying to convince your reader of your **point of view.** You explain your side of an argument and support it with facts and examples.

State your **argument**—or your view on the topic.

"No gum in school!" wouldn't teachers like to stop reminding their students about this random rule? I think students should be allowed to chew gum in school. Chewing gum can actually help students in several ways.

2. Give **reasons** to support your argument. When you can, provide **evidence** to back up your reasons. If you're not sure how many reasons to write about, aim for three. Give each reason its own paragraph.

Chewing gum may actually help students learn. Some studies have shown that chewing gum helps people concentrate. There's no doubt that teachers want students to be able to concentrate in class.

Chewing gum also helps you not feel hungry. When lunch is hours away or you need a snack to get through the day, gum can help you feel full so you can get back to your schoolwork.

Chewing gum makes students feel more happy and relaxed. We all know teachers don't want students to feel stressed at school.

3 State the **opposing argument** and give reasons why it's not correct. (You can skip this step if that's what works best for your assignment.)

Teachers say gum is messy. Of course, I agree that kids should get in trouble if they make a mess with gum. Give detentions for gum messes, and make kids clean it up. Teachers say gum is distracting. But lots of things are distracting, and we can't get rid of all of them. Maybe gum can help kids practice not getting distracted.

4 **Restate** your argument.

There are good reasons for letting students chew gum in school. Gum helps kids concentrate, it keeps them from getting hungry, and it helps them relax. If students are responsible about gum messes, I think teachers won't regret choosing to let students chew.

persuasive power words

The words you choose can add power to your persuasion at each point along the way.

Use these phrases in your writing to win over the audience to your side of the argument:

> It's clear that . . .
> It's easy to understand that . . .
> We all need . . .
> We all want . . .
> Everyone knows that . . .
> Most people believe that . . .
> No one doubts that . . .
> Studies show that . . .
> Research states that . . .

Make sure your readers follow your argument with these useful transitions:

> Furthermore, . . .
> In addition, . . .
> In the same way, . . .
> What's more, . . .

Use these phrases to refute the opposing argument:

> Perhaps . . . but . . .
> Some might claim . . . however . . .
> Sometimes . . . but . . .
> Even though . . . it's still clear that . . .

Use these phrases to conclude or summarize your argument:

> To sum it up, . . .
> Considering these reasons, . . .
> For the reasons above, . . .
> As I have shown, . . .

POST IT!
Write better letters to persuade, give thanks, ask questions, or just say hello.

April 15, 2017

JRA

Principal Maria Swanson
Mighty Oak School
123 Acorn Lane
Hometown, Wisconsin 55555

Dear Principal Swanson,

I'm writing to ask you to consider adding time to lunch period. Did you know that by the time I get through the lunch line, I usually have less than 10 minutes to gulp down my food? We students would truly appreciate having an extra 10 minutes to relax and eat our meals at a normal pace.

School lunch can be stressful for kids. It's hard enough to figure out where to sit! Knowing I have to eat in a rush or be hungry all after-noon makes me dread lunch period.

I understand that the school day lasts only a certain amount of time. I'd never expect you to take time away from classes. I, for one, would be happy to give up a few minutes of recess for a longer lunch.

Sincerely,

Jillian Reddy

Jillian Reddy
5th grader

Include the **date** on all your letters—even informal notes.

The **heading** of your letter gives the name and address of the person you're writing to (called the *recipient*). Informal notes to friends and family can skip this step. For more formal letters, include your own name and address above the recipient's so he or she can send you a reply.

The **greeting** usually starts with "Dear," followed by the name of the person to whom you're writing, and then a comma.

The **body** of your letter contains your message.

In the **closing** and **signature**, sign off with a final sentiment such as "Sincerely," "Yours truly," or "Your friend," and give your name. If your letter is typed, leave space to sign it by hand above your printed name. Include your title, too, if it's appropriate.

DIGITAL DOS AND DON'TS

What happens when the digital world and your schoolwork collide? Choose what you would do in each situation.

1 You need to e-mail your teacher to ask about an assignment that you don't quite understand. Your message begins . . .

a. dont get UR hmwrk, send more deets pls.

b. Dear Ms. Willowby, I have a few questions about tonight's homework. First, I'm not sure . . .

2 Your teacher wants you to use the school website to post messages about class topics and assignments. Great! You hop online to . . .

a. shoot your teacher a message about the movie you saw yesterday. You know he'd love it!

b. post a link to a website where you found information that helps with your homework.

3 You and your pals love sharing funny pet photos on Picture Pop, a new social media tool. You know your teacher loves dogs, so you . . .

a. find her Picture Pop account and share a photo of your pup along with all of your friends' comments.

b. decide to use some Picture Pop pet pics for a class project on dogs.

"don't get UR hmwrk send more deets"

4 Your art teacher stayed after school to help you work on a challenging project. You decide to thank her with . . .

a. a text message—"thx teach!!!"— with a photo of your completed homework attached.

b. a straightforward e-mail saying how much you appreciate her help.

5 Your teacher is a total techie. She requires you to turn in your homework online and take all your tests on in-class laptops. For your next assignment, a persuasive essay, you fill your writing with . . .

a. texting abbreviations and emojis. Your teacher knows the code.

b. strong arguments supported by facts you found through the library's online databases.

Answers

Did you choose any **a's?** Beware! Computers, tablets, and phones make communicating easier than ever. However, the way you write online depends on the person you're writing to. You speak differently to your friends than you do to your teachers, and it's best to write differently as well. Texting shorthand, emojis, and casual language don't belong in homework or communications with teachers. Also, make sure digital messages you send to your teacher are related to school. Last, even if you love your teacher, don't ask to connect on social media. Teachers need a private life, too!

REPORTS and RESEARCH WRITING

Plan and polish nonfiction and informational writing.

BETTER BOOK REPORTS

Follow the path to your perfect read.

Ask for book suggestions. Talk to friends and family. Check the library website and book review sites for recommendations. Ask a librarian! He or she can guide you toward the perfect report-ready book.

Check the details of your assignment. Can you choose any book, or do you need to pick from a particular list, author, or genre such as historical fiction or biography?

Think about authors you like. Do you have a favorite book series? Can you read the next book?

LIBRARY

EB WHITE

PILKEY

WILDER

PennyPacker

Sendak

TOLKIEN

ROWLING

Consider different genres: realistic fiction, fantasy, mystery, fairy tale, biography, memoir, history, informational, graphic novel, and more. Books that have won an award, such as the Newbery Medal, are great choices, too.

WARNING

Read the Book!

Teachers know if you didn't. You'll know, too. Sure, it's easy to find book summaries online. But a book report should give *your* impressions of the book, not another person's. Plus, relying on a book summary could be plagiarism.

Know how much time you have. Make sure you can finish the book and write about it before your report is due.

Relax and read! (And take notes, too!)

WRITE WHAT YOU READ

Take notes, and then answer questions to craft your report.

When you're reading a book for a report, take notes. Write interesting details about the book in a notebook, and use sticky notes to mark important passages on the pages. Keep track of . . .

People: What characters are important? Why? How do they change in the story?

Action: For fiction, what's the plot? What problems come up, and how are they solved? For nonfiction, what happens? Or, what are you supposed to learn?

Theme: What are the "big ideas" in your book? What do the characters learn?

Favorite quotes: Mark your favorite lines and passages. Try to include a quote or two (or three!) in your book report.

BEYOND BOOK BASICS

Try out one of these creative formats for your next book report!

Create a comic-book version of the book.	Write and perform a skit based on a key scene.	Design your own book jacket with a front cover illustration, "I loved it!" quotes on the back, and a description of the book for the flap.	Dress up as your book's main character to deliver your report.

After you read, answer these questions as you write up your report:

Who wrote the book, and what is the title?

Where and **when** does the book take place?

Who are the main characters if the book is fiction, or who is it about if the book is nonfiction?

What is the book about? For fiction, what is the main action of the plot? For nonfiction, what is the subject? What happens? What does the book teach?

How is the book written? Describe the voice. Did you enjoy how the author used language? What did you notice?

How do you feel about the book? Did you love it? Hate it? Feel it was just okay? Why?

Why is the book important? Explain the book's main themes or big ideas. What did you learn?

Create a diorama of a favorite scene.

Write a letter to the author explaining what you learned and what you liked about the book. Remember to include your questions, too.

Rewrite the ending. Imagine the book turned out a different way. What else might happen?

The End

research RULES

Plan, Look for information, Organize facts and ideas,
and Write your draft to **PLOW** your way to a great report!

Plan

Get ready to research by brainstorming ideas and
questions about your topic. List the information that
you already know and what you want to find out.

topic	What do I already know?	What do I want to find out?
Canoeing	❀ takes teamwork if two in boat ❀ beginners should <u>not</u> stand ❀ how to do different strokes ❀ parts of boat	❀ who used canoes first? ❀ Have canoes been important in history? ❀ what are some different ways people use canoes today?

Look for information

Search for answers to the questions you brainstormed. For short reports, you may find all the info you need in just a couple of sources, but research papers require you to dig deeper. Look in different kinds of sources—books, websites, encyclopedias, magazines—and ask a librarian where you can find more.

After you gather your sources, read them and take notes. Keep track of your sources! Use a notebook or computer to record ideas and information from books, magazine articles, and other references. Print out online information and highlight important facts. Keep track of what information comes from what source. Remember to paraphrase, or put ideas in your own words. If you include a direct quote from a source, mark it as a quote.

Compare the information you find, and use it to start forming your own conclusions.

from Britannica School (website)
— Canoes work in shallow and deep water.
— Canoes were the first real boats made and used by early humans.
— Canoes were made by early people all over the world, all the way back to the stone age.
— quote: "The modern recreation and sport of canoeing was organized by Scottish sportsman John MacGregor."

from Boat (book)
— Native Americans made early canoes using tree bark.
— Dugout canoes were made by early people by hollowing out a log.
— quote: "Like the skin on an animal, the skin of a tree—its bark—makes a watertight boat." p. 12

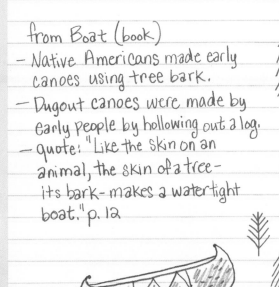

Organize

Facts and Ideas

Now that you have your information, review it carefully to choose the best way to organize it in your report. Create an outline of your information using one of these methods:

Argument
Make a claim or argument, and use facts to support it. Begin and end with your strongest or most interesting pieces of evidence.

Chronology
Organize your information by the order it happens in time. This method works well for reports on history topics.

like this

Cause and Effect
Describe a problem or question. Explain what causes the problem and what results from it. Offer solutions or answers.

Compare and Contrast
Show how two subjects or ideas are alike or different.

CANOEING (organized chronologically)

Canoes not just for fun. Also important in history.

1. Canoes earliest form of boat
   - helped people travel and collect food
   - made from different materials

2. Canoes important for exploration
   - early European explorers in North America

3. Canoeing became more recreational
   - Starting in the 1860s, people went canoeing to admire nature
   - Still the same today. Canoeing is popular recreation among nature lovers.

4. Canoeing is for everyone
   - not too expensive
   - easy to learn

Write
your draft

Writing a report is a lot like telling a story. You create a beginning, a middle, and an end. You support your ideas with evidence so your story is convincing. You write so your readers can follow your thoughts along the way.

The Beginning

Begin by telling readers the main idea of your report and why that idea is interesting or important. Avoid starting with "I am going to tell you . . ." Instead, try a quote, question, or interesting fact to grab your readers' attention.

<u>All About Canoes</u>

Did you know that canoes are the first real boats that people ever built? Scientists that are called "archaeologists" have found pieces of old canoes that were carved from logs at least 8,000 years ago! You might think canoes are just for fun, but canoes have changed history, too.

The Middle

Fill the middle of your report with evidence supporting your main idea. The evidence can be reasons, examples, or facts. Give three or four of them.

At least as early as the Stone Age, people made canoes to travel and to help them collect food. Around the world, people used different materials to build their canoes. Some Native Americans covered wood frames with tree bark. Others used animal skins.

European explorers in North America copied Native Americans and built canoes to travel around the many waterways they discovered . . .

Canoeing is exciting and fun, but canoes have also changed history. They allowed early people to collect food and travel, and they were used to explore new lands. For more than 150 years, canoeing has also been popular as recreation. In a canoe, you can get in touch with history yourself. You can experience the wilderness as people have for thousands of years!

The End

In the end or conclusion of your report, restate your main idea. Then summarize the evidence and answer remaining questions. To add strength and interest to the ending, restate the main point in a new way or remind readers of a cool fact.

QUIZ source SLEUTH!

Spot the stronger source in each pair.

1 You're writing about your favorite author. You'd trust information from . . .

a website created by someone who says she's the author's "biggest fan ever!"

an encyclopedia database you access at your school library.

2 You're writing a current events report on your city's election for mayor. You'd rely on facts from . . .

a newspaper article.

a campaign advertisement promoting one of the candidates.

3 You're working on a persuasive essay to convince people to visit your favorite state park. You'd use information from . . .

the official government website for the park.

a website with beautiful photos from the park but no author or sponsor as far as you can tell.

4 You're researching a science paper on circuit boards. You'd refer to . . .

a science textbook that was published last year.

a book about circuits published 20 years ago.

5 You're writing about trends in baking. You'd include information from . . .

a conversation with your brother, who loves to eat cupcakes.

an interview with a professional chef.

answers

Did you choose all **blues?** Congrats—you know how to track down reliable source material! Did you pick any **reds?** You're not alone. The clues to solid sources can be difficult to spot. The next time you're trying to detect whether a source is reliable, ask yourself these questions:

Is this source known for being accountable for its information?

Books, encyclopedias, and newspaper articles are almost always checked for accuracy before they're printed. Information on government and academic websites gets checked, too. Fan sites and sites designed to sell products may be less reliable.

Is the information in this source fact or opinion?

You can use both! Just make sure you know the difference. A campaign ad for the candidate for mayor may not be as reliable or straightforward as a news article about him or her.

Is the author of the information an expert in the topic?

University professors, researchers, and journalists need to support the information they present with facts they can prove.

Is the information current?

Scientific information and news stories should be as current as possible for the most up-to-date facts on changing subjects.

BIBLIOGRAPHY BASICS

Give credit, and show where you found your information.

Teachers usually give you a bibliography form so you can fill in the blanks with the details they want about each kind of source. The form might look like this.

Mr. Troutflower's Bibliography Sheet

Project Title: My Summer Canoeing
Name: Margaux Drew-Camus

BOOK
Author's last name, first name. Book Title. Where published: Publishing company, copyright year. (Page numbers you read)

Fledging, Lena. A Smart Girl's Guide to Canoes. Midtown, WI: Live & Learn, 2014. (Pages 5-12, 37)

WEBPAGE OR WEBSITE
"Title of Page or Site." URL. (Date you found it)

"Life on the River." www.lifeontheblueplanet.org/rivers. (October 29, 2016)

ONLINE DATABASE OR ENCYCLOPEDIA
"Article or Page Title." Database Title. Date published. (Date you found it)

"Canoes." Universe Encyclopedia Online. 2004. (October 27, 2016)

PRINT ENCYCLOPEDIA
"Article Title." Encyclopedia Title, volume, page numbers. Date published.

"Boats." Earth Book, volume A, pages 194-195. 2013.

MAGAZINE OR NEWSPAPER ARTICLE
"Article Title." Magazine or Newspaper Title, page numbers. Date published.

"Evidence of Early Canoes Found." The Highland Post, pages 3-4. July 10, 2015.

PERSONAL INTERVIEW
Last name of person interviewed, first name. Personal interview. Date of interview.

Boat, Rocky. Personal interview. October 10, 2016.

TESTING, TESTING

If you fear short-answer and essay questions, follow this formula to ace your exams!

When teachers include short-answer and essay questions on tests, they want to see if you know and understand the material you've studied. They're also finding out if you can communicate your ideas about it.

 1 Make sure you're clear on what each question asks. Watch for and underline phrases such as "list reasons," "give examples," and "explain why or why not," which tell you what form your answer should take.

> <u>List at least three reasons why</u> American colonists wanted independence from England. <u>Explain</u> your answer.

2 Note the main idea you need in your answer. Jot it down on scratch paper.

MAIN IDEA:
American colonists wanted independence from England ~~because they liked their new country~~ ~~because they were tired of the English way of life~~ because they felt they weren't being treated fairly by England

3 Next, on your scratch paper, list the facts and ideas that support your main idea.

> —unfair taxes and laws
> —no say in their government
> —little control over their property

4 Write out your answer. Introduce your main idea in the first sentence. Don't forget to include transition words to guide the teacher through your ideas. Restate your main idea at the end of your answer.

List at least three reasons why American colonists wanted independence from England. Explain your answer.

American colonists wanted independence from England because they felt they were not treated fairly by the king and England's government.
First . . .
Also . . .
Finally . . .
In the end, the colonists fought for independence to gain freedom from unfair treatment and a voice in their government.

5 Check your spelling, punctuation, capitalization, and grammar when you reread your answer to make sure it makes sense. And be sure you indent every paragraph.

PENCIL POINT

Not sure what to say? Give as much information as you can, and you'll still earn some points. You might even find that once you start, the process of writing will spark your memory! Just do your best.

REVISING AND EDITING

When you're done,
you've just begun.

make the grade

What do teachers really want from your writing?

 1 Teachers want you to write as much as you can for every assignment. Longer always means better.

        TRUE   FALSE

 2 The more complex, long, and flowery the words you use in your writing, the higher the grade your teacher will give you.

        TRUE   FALSE

 3 Teachers expect any writing you turn in to be totally error-free. No spelling or grammar mistakes, ever!

        TRUE   FALSE

4 When teachers ask you to turn in a first draft, your writing had better be pretty polished. Why else would they want to see your work?

        TRUE   FALSE

 5 Teachers expect you to edit your writing all on your own. Editing help from your classmates, your parents, or the teacher herself is strictly off-limits!

        TRUE   FALSE

 6 Teachers expect you to figure out writing assignments on your own. No questions, please! After all, you're the author.

        TRUE   FALSE

7 Teachers don't expect your writing to be as good as what you read in books. But they do want you to do your best!

TRUE   FALSE

answers

1 False — Your teachers want you to follow directions. Stick to the word, paragraph, or page counts in your assignment. Aim for quality, not quantity.

2 False — Teachers love a good vocabulary, but they want you to write with language you understand that expresses your ideas clearly.

3 False — Teachers expect you to check your work for spelling and grammar errors. But everyone makes mistakes—and mistakes are part of learning.

4 False — Teachers ask for a draft to see if you're making progress. The point of drafting and editing is to change writing to make it a bit better with each revision. Your first draft isn't supposed to be perfect.

5 False — Teachers hope you learn that writing can be a collaborative process. It's great to get input from others to make sure your writing communicates your ideas clearly.

6 False — Teachers want you to understand assignments. If you have a question, ask!

7 TRUE — Teachers know learning to write well is a long process. The more you practice, the better you will become.

CHANGE FOR THE BETTER

In the writing process, reviewing and revising are as important as brainstorming ideas and crafting your draft.

IDEAS AND PURPOSE

Do you remember these important questions?

1 What's the main idea I want my writing to share?

2 What's the purpose or job of my writing?

Your first task when you revise a writing assignment is to make sure the main idea is clear. Second, make sure your writing does the job you want it to do. Does it persuade, inform, or entertain—or do two or all three of these jobs? Read your draft carefully to see if it gives the message you want and does the job you want. If not, you can change it. Now's the time.

Next, make sure your writing tells a story that your reader can follow. Is there a clear beginning, middle, and end? Does it flow easily from one part to the next? (Hint: Do you use transition words like the ones on page 38?) Don't be afraid to rearrange the order of sentences or paragraphs to make your story flow better. If your draft doesn't make sense to you, your reader may not understand your meaning either.

Now check to make sure each paragraph contains one clear idea. If a paragraph is overloaded, break it down into shorter ones.

STYLE

Check in again with these important questions: Does the voice of your draft fit your main idea and the job you want your writing to do? Does your writing sound serious if you're talking about something serious? Is your writing light and cheerful if you're describing something fun or funny?

Is your voice *consistent*? Does it all sound like it comes from the same person? Aim for the same voice from start to finish.

Search your draft for repeated words and phrases. Do you use the same words over and over again? If so, swap in some alternatives. Look for variety in your sentence lengths, too, so they have a nice rhythm between long and short.

MAKING CUTS

Ouch! It can be painful to cut part of your draft. You worked hard to get those words on the page! But deleting the problem parts of your writing sometimes works better—and is much easier—than trying to fix the problem parts. Remember that words are words, not rare gems. If they don't help you communicate your main idea, choose new ones or lose them altogether. Here's a good rule of thumb: When in doubt, leave it out!

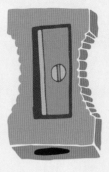

PENCIL POINT

Back it up! When you write on a computer, it's especially easy to make cuts and to compare older drafts with new versions. Just save the older drafts of your document, and name each draft so that you know which is which, such as **Canoes (draft 2)** or **Canoes (May 12).** You can always put the words back in the document if you change your mind.

MS. FIX-IT

Small errors weaken words, so edit the **mechanics** to give your writing strength and power.

SPELLING

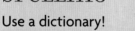

Use a dictionary!

If writing on a computer, use the spell-check program, but don't rely on it to catch every misspelling.

Know your trouble spots. Double-check spellings you're unsure of.

Grammar

Don't use casual language for essays, reports, and other formal writing assignments.

Write in complete sentences.

No **fragments,** like this one.

punctuation

End each sentence with the right punctuation: a period, a question mark—or an exclamation point!

Use commas to separate items in a list, to separate clauses in a sentence, and to introduce quotations.

> She said, "I'm almost done!"

Use apostrophes to form **possessives:**
> that girl's sister
> her parents' room
> the children's toys

and **contractions:**
> they won't wait
> she'll be ready

Format

Follow all formatting directions your teacher has given you.

Indent new paragraphs.

Double-space typed writing. You can skip lines in handwritten work, too, for neatness and to leave room for your teacher's comments.

Make sure to include your name and the date!

capitalization

Begin sentences with capital letters.

Capitalize the names of people, cities, states, and countries.

Capitalize days, months, and holidays.

Capitalize important words in titles.

pencil point

If you're unsure about grammar, punctuation, or other mechanics, check a **style manual** or ask your teacher for help.

SPELL-CHECK

How many spelling errors can you spot?

Last Febuary, I attended a truely wierd marrage.
I am not embarassed to say that I go to quiet alot of
weddings. I went with my freind Arianna so I wouldn't
be lonly. Everything was beutiful accept the whether.
Lightening struck the alter! I had a grate time, thow. I
should get out my stationary to right a thank-you note
for the invitation.

ANSWERS

Last February, I attended a truly weird
marriage. I am not embarrassed to say
that I go to quite a lot of weddings. I went
with my friend Arianna so I wouldn't be
lonely. Everything was beautiful except
the weather. Lightning struck the altar!
I had a great time, though. I should get out
my stationery to write a thank-you note
for the invitation.

Great Grammar

Complete each sentence with the correct word to see if you're a grammar goddess!

1. Izzy and me   I judged a pie contest.

2. The contestants gave their pies to Izzy and me   I.

3. We were suppose   supposed to taste every pie.

4. It was really hard to decide if one pie was better than   then another pie.

5. I love cherry pie. It's   Its my favorite!

6. It was difficult to choose a winner among   between all twelve pies.

7. We decided we would half   have to give the prize to the cherry pie after all.

8. After the contest, we made sure to return each pie dish to it's   its owner.

Answers

QUICK FIXES

Look out for these common grammar errors.

Use **I** for the **subject** of the sentence or the object of a **"to be"** verb:
> She and I ride the bus.
> My brother and I love cake.
> It is I.

Use **me** as the object of a **preposition** or **verb** other than "to be":
> She gave the flowers to my mother and me.
> Between you and me, the roses were the prettiest.
> The teacher chose Winnie and me to read first.

It's is the contraction for "it is":
> It's fun to play piano.

Its is the possessive form of "it":
> The cat licked its fur clean.

Use **between** when referring to two items:
> I sat between my two friends.

Use **among** when referring to more than two items:
> I ordered pizza from among the many entrees on the menu.

Their is the possessive form of "them":
> My parents celebrated their anniversary.

They're is the contraction for "they are":
> They're going out to a fancy restaurant to celebrate.

There is an adverb that refers to a location:
> My parents were married there.

You're is the contraction for "you are":
> You're my best friend.

Your is the possessive form of "you":
> Wear your jacket in the rain.

EDITING DECODER
Learn a secret language!

Your teacher reviews your essay draft, but do you know what she's telling you? Use this guide to understand what all those marks mean.

EDITING AND PROOFREADING MARKS

delete — Sometimes ~~every once in a while~~ writers use extra words.

close up — Take out the words that are extra and not needed.

insert — Add letter, punctuation marks or words.

lower case /lc — Don't Use capital letters Where they are not Needed.

capitalize ≡ cap — Use uppercase letters for names, such as ms. winterspoon.

new paragraph — Start a new paragraph.

spelling SP — Circle misspelled (wurds)

transpose — Switch the of order words or lettres.

insert a period — Statements end with a period

keep original text ~~stet~~ — Oops! I made a mistake.
Stet

MAKING THE MOST OF REVIEWS

Use comments from others to improve your writing.

Make all mechanics changes that your teacher suggests.

If your classmate makes a mechanics change you're unsure of, check with your teacher.

Does your reader suggest cuts? Try them. Read your draft without the cut material. Is it better?

Pay attention to places where a reader says she doesn't understand something. If she can't follow your writing, rewrite, add, or cut to make it clearer.

Does your reader ask for more information? If you have it, give it. If you don't, consider cutting out the part that raises an unanswered question.

Remember, you're the writer. In the end, you are the one who makes the decisions.

THE FINAL EXAM

Before you turn in a writing assignment, complete this checklist to make sure it will pass with the highest marks.

✔ Is the main idea of my writing clear?

✔ Does my writing persuade, inform, or entertain the way I want it to?

✔ Do I start with my main idea and follow it through from beginning to middle to end?

✔ Does the voice of my writing fit with my main idea?

✔ Do I use language that is both interesting and clear?

✔ Did I format my assignment correctly?

✔ Did I check the assignment one last time to make sure I followed all of the directions?

✔ Did I check for spelling errors?

✔ Did I check for correct grammar?

✔ Did I check punctuation?

✔ Did I check capitalization?

WORD PLAY

Host your own
writer's workshop.

Draft Exchange

Do your friends love to write?

The next time you're working on a big assignment, invite a group of pals to review drafts, spark new ideas, and write together. Start by sharing drafts of whatever writing assignment you're working on. Partner up, trade drafts, and read what your partner has written. Then . . .

1 Try to answer these questions about your partner's draft:

- Is the main idea of the writing clear to you? If not, how could the writer make her main idea shine through?

- What is the writer's goal? Is she trying to persuade, inform, or entertain? Is she doing more than one of these? All three? How?

- Can you follow the writing from beginning to end? If not, where do you get confused?

2 Check the draft for mechanics: spelling, grammar, punctuation, capitalization, and the right formatting. Mark mistakes where you see them.

3 As you offer suggestions to your partner, be specific. Instead of writing "confusing" next to a paragraph you didn't understand, say what's unclear. Instead of crossing out words you didn't like, ask what she hoped those words would do. Instead of writing "good," say which ideas interested you or which phrases pleased you— and why.

When your draft work is done, it's time for some **FUN!**

Pencil Point

Always find something good to say—and try to make at least half of your comments positive.

LOADED DICE

Roll your way to super stories with this dice game!

1. You'll need a six-sided die, a notebook for each girl, and pens or pencils. Each girl rolls the die three times. In her own notebook, she writes down the numbers she rolls and the story prompt that her rolls create, following this list:

First roll chooses a main character:

= Supergirl

= a talking cat

= a funny grandma

= the President

= your younger sister or brother

= a monster who's easily frightened

Third roll selects the setting:

= in the woods

= on another planet

= at your house

= at your school

= in Hollywood

= in the attic of a haunted house

Second roll determines the plot or action of the story:

= takes a vacation

= plans a party

= enters a contest

= tells a lie

= has a fight with a friend

= learns to play the piano

For example, a girl who rolls 2, then 1, then 5 creates this story starter:

A talking cat takes a vacation in Hollywood . . .

2. After each player has rolled, everyone writes about her own story prompt for 7 minutes. When time is up, each girl shares her favorite part of what she wrote.

secret story

What happens when everyone adds her own twist to the same story? Play this game to find out!

1 You will need one blank notebook and a pen or pencil. Begin with a story prompt that's been chosen by the group. Roll a prompt from the Loaded Dice game, choose a prompt from pages 54–55, or come up with your own. Write the prompt on the first page of the blank notebook.

2 One girl begins the story by turning the page and writing a paragraph inspired by the prompt. When she's done, she turns to the next blank page in the notebook, rewrites the final sentence of her paragraph at the top of the page, and passes the notebook to the next writer.

3 The next writer continues the story based on the sentence at the top of her page. Use only the front sides of the notebook pages so that each player's full paragraph is hidden from the next player. Keep passing the notebook until every girl has a turn to write. No peeking at what has been written before your turn! Write based only on the starting prompt and the sentence at the top of your page.

4 When everyone is finished, have one player read the story out loud to the group.

POETRY SLAM

See who's quick with rhythm and rhyme in a poetry performance.

1 Each player gets paper and a pen or pencil. One player chooses a topic. She can select whatever she likes: cats, birthday cake, little brothers, snow, the school principal—any topic will work.

2 Next, set a timer for 3 minutes. In that time, all players try to write a few lines of poetry about the topic.

3 When time is up, the players take turns reading what they have written.

4 After everyone reads, players vote for their favorite poem performance. The player with the most votes picks the topic for the next round!

KIND WORDS

End your writer's workshop on a positive note.

 1 To begin, all players sit in a circle. You will need pens or pencils and a large blank note card for each person. Each girl writes her name on one side of the note card and passes her card to the left.

 2 Each girl uses her best writing to craft a compliment about the girl whose name appears on the front of the card passed to her. When all players are done writing, pass the cards to the left again. Keep passing until each person has written on each card and receives her original card back, now filled with kind words.

 Don't forget to tell your friends what creative, thoughtful, inspiring writers they are!

LEARNING TO WRITE WELL IS A LOT LIKE LEARNING TO CANOE.

You learn the basics.

You learn the strokes.

You practice.

And in the end, writing can take you ANYWHERE you want to go!

What are your best writing tips?
How do you succeed at school writing assignments?

Write to us!
School RULES! Writing Editor
American Girl
8400 Fairway Place
Middleton, WI 53562

All comments and suggestions received by American Girl may be used without compensation or acknowledgment. We're sorry, but photos can't be returned.

Here are some other American Girl® books you might like.

Each sold separately. Find more books online at americangirl.com.

Parents, request a FREE catalog at **americangirl.com/catalog.**
Sign up at **americangirl.com/email** to receive the latest news and exclusive offers.

Discover online games, quizzes, activities,
and more at **americangirl.com/play**